BETTER TOGETHER: ANIMAL GROUPS

KANGAROO MOBS

by Karen Latchana Kenney

Ideas for Parents and Teachers

Pogo Books let children practice reading informational text while introducing them to nonfiction features such as headings, labels, sidebars, maps, and diagrams, as well as a table of contents, glossary, and index.

Carefully leveled text with a strong photo match offers early fluent readers the support they need to succeed.

Before Reading

- "Walk" through the book and point out the various nonfiction features. Ask the student what purpose each feature serves.
- Look at the glossary together. Read and discuss the words.

Read the Book

- Have the child read the book independently.
- Invite him or her to list questions that arise from reading.

After Reading

- Discuss the child's questions. Talk about how he or she might find answers to those questions.
- Prompt the child to think more. Ask: What did you know about kangaroos before reading this book? What more would you like to learn about them after reading it?

Pogo Books are published by Jump!
5357 Penn Avenue South
Minneapolis, MN 55419
www.jumplibrary.com

Library of Congress Cataloging-in-Publication Data

Names: Kenney, Karen Latchana, author.
Title: Kangaroo mobs / by Karen Latchana Kenney.
Description: Pogo books edition.
Minneapolis, MN: Jump!, Inc., [2020]
Series: Better together: animal groups
Audience: Age 7-10.
Includes bibliographical references and index.
Identifiers: LCCN 2019007080 (print)
LCCN 2019007903 (ebook)
ISBN 9781641288507 (ebook)
ISBN 9781641288491 (hardcover : alk. paper)
Subjects: LCSH: Kangaroos–Behavior–Juvenile literature.
Animal societies–Juvenile literature.
Classification: LCC QL737.M35 (ebook)
LCC QL737.M35 K458 2020 (print)
DDC 599.2/22–dc23
LC record available at https://lccn.loc.gov/2019007080

Editor: Jenna Trnka
Designer: Jenna Casura

Photo Credits: JohnCarnemolla/iStock, cover; FLPA/Alamy, 1; Rabsanity/Shutterstock, 3; blickwinkel/Alamy, 4; Arco Images GmbH/Alamy, 5; Alexius Sutandio/Shutterstock, 6-7tl; quentinjlang/iStock, 6-7tr; ChameleonsEye/Shutterstock, 6-7bl; CraigRJD/iStock, 6-7br; Juniors/SuperStock, 8-9; Viktor Posnov/Alamy, 10-11; Wendy Sinclair/iStock, 11; SA Tourist/Shutterstock, 12; Breathes/Shutterstock, 13; Martin Willis/Minden Pictures/SuperStock, 14-15; Ernie Janes/Alamy, 16-17; Steve Downer/Age Fotostock, 18; Wonderly Imaging/Shutterstock, 19; Ilia Torlin/Shutterstock, 20-21; miwa-in-oz/Shutterstock, 23.

Printed in the United States of America at Corporate Graphics in North Mankato, Minnesota.

TABLE OF CONTENTS

CHAPTER 1

SAFETY IN NUMBERS

This **herbivore** stops **grazing**. Why? It hears something. Its ears move around to listen. Could it be danger?

The kangaroo thumps its feet on the ground. It warns the other members of its **mob**. They hear the thumps. They stand tall and look around, too. Then they all hop away!

There are four kinds of kangaroos. They are the western and eastern grey, antilopine, and red. Red kangaroos are the largest **marsupials** in the world. One can weigh up to 200 pounds (91 kilograms). They can grow to around six feet (1.8 meters) tall.

western grey kangaroo

eastern grey kangaroo

antilopine kangaroo

red kangaroo

Kangaroos live, eat, and sleep in groups called mobs. Some mobs are small. Others have more than 100 kangaroos!

Each mob lives in a certain area. This area is its **home range**. It has a good supply of food and water.

TAKE A LOOK!

All kinds of kangaroos live on Australia. Take a look where each kind lives! Eastern grey kangaroos live on Tasmania, too.

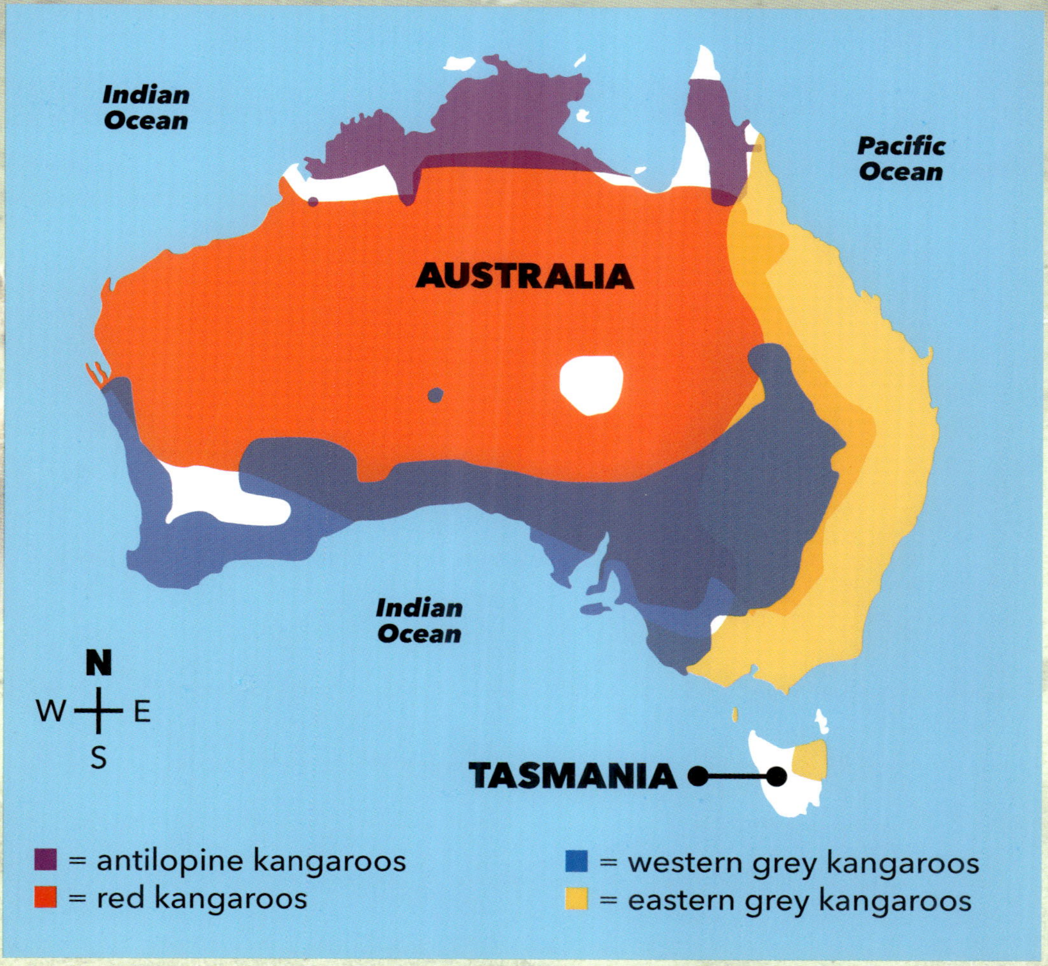

Many eyes and ears are in a mob. They all watch and listen for **predators**. Dingoes try to sneak up on them. Eagles try to eat **joeys**. If one hears something, it lets the others know. The news spreads quickly.

DID YOU KNOW?

How do kangaroos hear so well? Their ears are large. They move in different directions, too. They pick up many sounds.

dingo

CHAPTER 2

MOB LIFE

The largest, strongest male leads the mob.

He has to fight to keep his role. Other males want to be the leader. They try to prove they are strong. How? They lean back on their tails. They kick and box.

They fight to **mate** with the females. The mob has many females. Daughters stay with their mothers their whole lives.

Mothers **groom** their joeys. They pick dirt, sticks, and rocks out of their fur. Some adults groom each other, too. They use their teeth, tongues, and toes.

DID YOU KNOW?

Kangaroos touch noses and sniff each other. This creates strong **bonds** in the mob.

CHAPTER 3

NEW MOB LEADERS

Joeys keep the mob growing. A joey is just one inch (2.5 centimeters) long at birth! It crawls to its mother's pouch. It drinks her milk and grows.

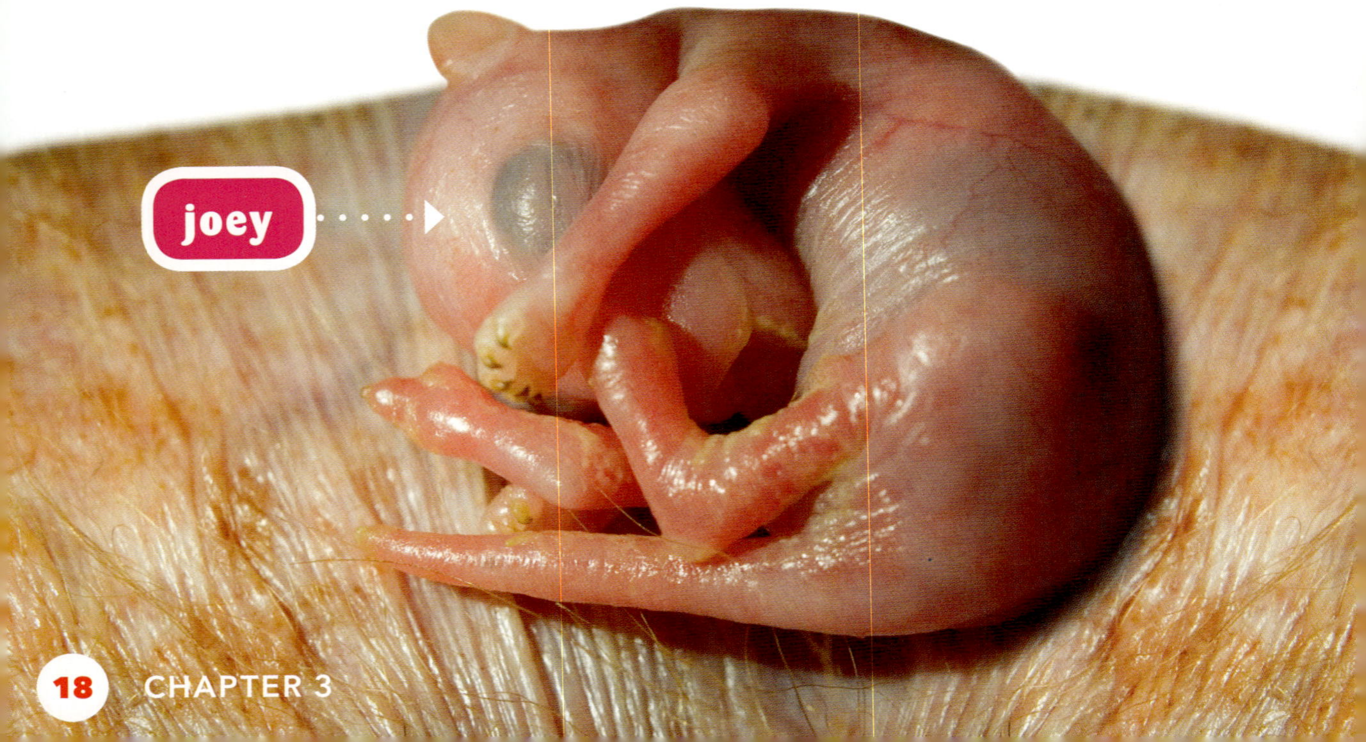

After around eight months, the joey leaves the pouch. But it stays close to its mother. It still drinks her milk.

Young joeys stay safe in the mob. They learn from older kangaroos. Male joeys practice fighting. When they are old enough, they leave the mob. They search for a new mob to join. One day, they may lead the mob, too.

DID YOU KNOW?

A kangaroo mother might have babies of different ages in her pouch. Mothers make two kinds of milk. One is for newborn babies. Another is for older joeys.

ACTIVITIES & TOOLS

TRY THIS!

MAKE A KANGAROO POUCH

Female kangaroos carry their joeys in their pouches. Try creating your own kangaroo pouch! Does a joey stay in when you hop around?

What You Need:

- an oversized T-shirt
- rope
- duct tape
- rubber bands
- a stuffed animal
- a friend

1. **Gather your materials and a friend to help you. Work together to think of ways you can create a pouch from an oversized T-shirt and the rest of your materials. Maybe one of you wears the shirt and folds up the bottom while the other tapes it up for a pouch. Try different ways.**
2. **After you have created your pouch, put your stuffed animal inside. Hop around the room. Does your joey stay in? If not, how could you improve your pouch? Can you think of other ways to create a kangaroo pouch?**

GLOSSARY

bonds: Close connections or strong feelings toward one another.

grazing: Feeding on grasses and plants.

groom: To take care of one's appearance by cleaning.

herbivore: An animal that only eat plants.

home range: An area over which an animal or group of animals lives.

joeys: Young kangaroos.

marsupials: Mammals whose females have a pouch for carrying young.

mate: To join together to produce babies.

mob: A group of kangaroos that lives together.

predators: Animals that hunt other animals for food.

INDEX

TO LEARN MORE

Finding more information is as easy as 1, 2, 3.

1. Go to www.factsurfer.com
2. Enter "kangaroomobs" into the search box.
3. Choose your book to see a list of websites.

FACT SURFER